I0802697

"A necessary read for any woman who is sick of depriving herself. Powers' poems trace a path from squeezing into the tired molds women are handed to unapologetically spilling over the top. *The Size of Your Joy* is an exploration of what women carry and a luminous reminder that there is always room for both our pain and our joy. Read this if you want to stop waiting to love your life."

— VICTORIA HUTCHINS
author of *Make Believe*

"Each poem felt like a generous treat, and how I wanted to savour them. Elise has such a gift for distilling the complexities of life, love, and longing into a few carefully chosen words. Her poetry is as powerful as it is gentle, the kind that lingers with you long after the page is turned. Her poems took me to so many places in so few lines, a true art, but also kind of magic."

— JESSICA URLICHS
author of *Beautiful Chaos*

"*The Size of Your Joy* traces what it is to be a woman in love with an impossible world. From girlhood to womanhood, this book reminds us what's worth holding onto."

— JOY SULLIVAN
author of *Instructions for Traveling West*

"In her debut collection, Elise Powers looks skyward to joy while reckoning with what she assumes to be her birthright of heartache. Indeed, she appears to discover playfulness like a puppy locating its tail for the first time."

— FOREWORD REVIEWS

"A tender exploration of womanhood, inheritance, and the brutal beauty woven through the everyday, *The Size of Your Joy* reminds us of the sacred ordinary. These are poems to return to again and again."

— DANIELLE COFFYN
author of *If Adam Picked the Apple*

"Elise's poetry feels like a conversation with an old friend. A friend that knows all of your dirty little secrets, your missteps and imperfections, your wants and needs. Her writing is intimate, warm, and honest; something for your heart to grasp when you're feeling too much."

— L. E. BOWMAN
author of *The Evolution of a Girl, What I Learned from the Trees,* and *Shapeshifter*

"The Size of Your Joy is as revelatory as it is relatable—a stunning, rich debut from a truly talented new voice that explores the gritty glory of modern womanhood with both wit and wisdom. From blood to bath time to breastfeeding and far beyond, Elise Powers makes magic of every topic she turns her attention toward."

— KELSEY LUCAS
creator of MotherSpeak (@motherspeak)

"Slow, gentle, and delicious. Elise Powers' voluptuous and deeply human collection of poetry takes its time traversing the tangled threads of love, loss, and desire that weave through the female lineage, connecting the women who came before to those who are still becoming. The Size of Your Joy is a love letter to the Imperfect Woman, and a reminder to eat your cake."

— SARAH
creator of Horrible Mean Bad Woman

"Elise Powers' words are utterly delicious. Her writing feels like an extended conversation with an old friend that takes place during the years when you've both grown up enough to care less about what others think and more about what you think, feel, and need. These poems are a must-read for any woman longing for joy in the midst of the messiness of life."

— MARISA RENEE LEE
author of *Grief is Love*

The Size of Your Joy

Elise M. Powers

"To the Woman at the Patisserie Who Turned Down Cake Because She Was 'Trying to Be Good'" is an after poem based on "To the Woman Crying Uncontrollably in the Next Stall" by Kim Addonizio

"Joy is Coming" is an after poem based on "To the Woman Crying Uncontrollably in the Next Stall" by Kim Addonizio

"Maybe You're Not Pretty. So What?" is after @horriblemeanbadwoman

"You Do Not Have To" is an after poem based on "Wild Geese" by Mary Oliver

"I Usually Avoid the News" is an after poem based on "Poem Not For My Son" by Ellen Bass

"Salad for Dinner" is an after poem based on "Dragonflies" by Danusha Laméris

"My Grandmother Says Wine Is Basically a Whole Food" is an after poem based on "My Mother Says Kissing a Man Without a Mustache is Like Eating Eggs Without Salt" by Joy Sullivan

"Did You Know We Literally Get One Wild and Precious Life?" is an after poem based on "Did You Know We Literally Get One Wild and Precious Life?" by Chloe Laws, which is an after poem of Mary Oliver's "The Summer Day."

"I Will Be Forgoing Hot Girl Summer" uses a phrase popularized by Megan Thee Stallion

"The First Sign of Civilization" is inspired by a popular anthropological anecdote often attributed to Margaret Mead.

Published by Central Avenue Poetry, an imprint of Central Avenue Marketing Ltd.
centralavenuepublishing.com

THE SIZE OF YOUR JOY: Poems

Trade Paperback: 978-1-77168-440-8
Ebook: 978-1-77168-441-5

Printed in the United States of America

1. POETRY / Women Authors 2. POETRY / Family

3 5 7 9 10 8 6 4 2

CONTENTS

I

II

III

IV

For my grandma and my grandmother,
who carried more than their fair share
and still passed down joy like an heirloom.

I

NOTHING BUT YES

My grandma kept the sugar
in a yellow nine-quart Tupperware tub
the size of Sunday stew,
tucked it under the cantilevered countertop
like treasure glistening in plain sight.
Sugar in coffee, sugar on toast,
sugar on a spoon straight into my mouth.
Barefoot on the linoleum,
I'd sneak mouthfuls
when no one was watching—
trap the sweet spark flat
to the roof of my mouth,
the thrill of not asking
like light behind closed eyes,
and grain by grain,
let it disappear
into nothing but yes,
into the joy of wanting something
and letting myself have it.

CRIMSON

No one warned me what would happen
when I *became a woman*.
That a slug of blood would ruin
my Christmas outfit—
how it was so crimson
it was black.
No one told me that I would coil my grief
tightly in my underwear, push it
to the shallow bottom of the bathroom trash,
how I'd bleed through
my toilet paper gusset over and over,
how I'd press the cotton blade between
my fingers like a key,
how it would slice my breath in two
at the blooming.
No one warned me that men
would toe my shadow down the sidewalk,
that strange eyes would settle
heavy and low as river rocks.
How eager the world is to pick the fruit
still green—to shuck a girl
like an oyster, drench her in vodka
and swallow her whole on the half shell,
as if the delicate meat of her exists
for anyone but herself.

THE FALL FROM GRACE

I remember the exact moment I began
to hate my body. I was ten or eleven
in my empty childhood bedroom,
wrestling a damp swimsuit over my skin—
skin that had been described as baby fat,
baby fat that I wasn't growing out of.
I was visiting my dad in the house
that used to be my home
and was now a mirage of it—
dust bunnies where toys once lived,
ghost-marked walls from frames
recently removed.
Everything had been stripped bare
and made uncanny
in the wake of divorce.
It was like I'd blinked and the orchard
was gone, a cherubim at the door
barring me from my bright green life,
from the girl I had been.
I remember standing there
in that hollowed-out house,
in that too-tight two-piece,
feeling like I was on the wrong side
of the gate, like I was looking in
at a home I could never return to—
the kind of place you only visit
to remember what you've lost.

FIELD TRIP

I was in the fourth grade
and we were walking in pairs.
The boy I liked was not far behind us.
I felt his eyes on me before I felt his hands.
Small, calculated invasions on our bodies
while our backs were turned,
while the chaperones weren't looking.
A squeeze here. A snap there. A push. A pull.
We giggled. Rolled our eyes.
It means they like us, my friend
whispered at my side,
that insidious way attention
of any kind feels like being chosen.
We tucked our discomfort into our sleeves.
Kept on moving so nothing could stick.
Even now, I can convince myself
it was just a field trip,
just a boy being stupid.
But the memory of this day
is a rock in my shoe,
and I can't kick it out.
Even now I'll feel it wedge itself under my heel
as I remember how many of us
learned to confuse being wanted
with being hunted.
How early the lesson begins,
and how long we carry it.

TO THE MAN WHO FIST-BUMPED MY DAUGHTER AFTER SHE SAID NO

Let me explain
it like this:
Today, you were
a drip.
And over time,
even the calmest
waters will carve
a canyon,
will turn solid rock
into surrender.
This is how it begins—
harmless as it might
have seemed,
you decided
you wanted
something
from her,
and you took it,
despite her
discomfort,
downturned eyes,
hands at her sides,
despite my voice—
directed at her,
but meant for you—
saying,
"You don't have to
if you don't want to."
One drop might
not seem like much,

but a thousand
small moments
where a girl is taught
that her *no*
is only a suggestion—
that's how the drips
become a current,
pulling her further
and further
from herself
until she's lost
at sea.

I WAS A CHILD

who learned too young
how to slacken my body to the undertow,
to let the waves claim me,
survive only by swimming sideways.
Even now, on dry land, my knees bend
to meet some invisible wake,
body still rocking from years
navigating the roughest seas.
I walk like Odysseus—
watching the horizon,
searching for the shape of home
in the shifting blue,
trusting the deck to hold me
only as much as the next wave allows,
waiting for the world to still,
longing for a distant home
that always stays just out of reach.

I HOLD MY BODY LIKE MEN HOLD FISH

Like something wild / to hook my fingers
into / dangle from my wrist / mount on a
wall / a thing to measure / for sport / admire
for its size / its luster / a prize when it pleases /
a waste when it doesn't / *this one put up
a fight!* / watch as it suffocates / under
scrutinizing eyes / mouth wide open / swallowing
nothing / picture perfect / like slipping water /
a thing to pin down / gutting knife in my back
pocket / catch, no release.

THINGS MEN FROM THE INTERNET HAVE SAID TO ME

can you show me your / you'd be hot if you / no
offense but you kinda look like / your feet are /
do you have a / be my sugar baby / I'd pay you
to / you should try / I bet you won't / you're so /
you look like / that looks like it / I hope your man
/ do you have any birthmarks / marry me /
where are you / you have sexy / do you have a /
what do you look like / please send me a pic of your /
I bet you like it / just so you know / honey, you're looking
pretty / I want you to / I thought about you while I /
I hate it when girls / you'd be a lot prettier if you

BAD LUCK

In those loaded-dice days of divorce,
after he threatened to bury her in the woods,
after she smashed the smoothtop into shards,
after he force-fed her the spark
and watched her burn with a beer in his hand,
after she patched each bruise like a leaky roof,
knowing the storm would come again,
my mother told me she had bad luck with men.
Bad luck, like a red sock washed with the whites,
a bird at the window tapping twice, spilled salt.
But you can't call it luck when the whole deck
is rigged—as if misfortune, not men,
put her in the fire.

SKY RATS

We carried them in our hands—
tied letters of love and war
to their paper-pink ankles.
They don't know
they're unwanted,
that they've become
iridescent burdens burrowed
in gutters we've lined with spikes
just for them.
They bob their heads,
coo at the feet that kick them away,
doing only as we taught them:
Return.
And isn't that the way of things?
The heart loves to outlive its welcome,
to circle the place it was last fed,
to make a meal out of crumbs.

RUNAWAY

I used to run away as a kid.
I'd pack my pink school backpack
full of toys and stand in the doorway,
a portal between what I knew
and what I didn't, and somberly
announce to the house that I was
leaving. Running away.
Right now. *For good!*
I'd inch down the sidewalk,
resisting the spur at my belly to look
back. All I wanted, it turns out,
was for someone to follow me,
tell me not to go.
That's all I want, still.

WISHING

I was an unhappy kid—
a child of divorce, raised in a generation
living in a state of aftershock.
My childhood felt like a leaf
caught in its own unfolding,
all tangled corners and shredded green.
Before my first period,
I was already depressed and anxious.
So much so that I developed a compulsion
for wishing—on candles, fountains, 11:11,
eyelashes, the rare (and promising) shooting star—
for happiness, as if it were something I'd find
buried in the chip aisle,
carry home swinging from the crook of my elbow
in a plastic grocery bag.
There were flashes of it—
pink cake, ice skates, movie theater laughter.
I knew happiness like a swimmer knows the shore:
arms outstretched, desperate for solid ground.
I realize now I couldn't have picked happiness out of a crowd—
only knew it by the way it brushed past me.
And still, all these years later, I catch myself wishing:
for a little more time before the cake goes stale,
the pond warms to slush, the movie ends.

CALIFORNIA

My little car lurches to a screaming stop
in the middle lane,
the road a blurred current
of red and silver—veins pulsing
beneath the skin of the world.
We hold our breath as the little doe's back legs
buckle from a cracking force
so loud it makes my teeth ache,
the car to our left striking her square in the head
as she tries to cross six lit-up lanes
of Pacific Coast Highway.
I think about yesterday,
when my sister had her first panic attack.
How her breath seized without warning—
how we pulled over in a Panera parking lot
and called an ambulance,
how we could do nothing
but will her lungs to expand,
how she told me later she thought
her heart had given out.
Now both my feet press the brakes flat to the floor,
my sister's hands covering her nose and mouth,
and we sit together again in helplessness,
watching this gentle creature twitch toward death,
half in our lane, half in the next,
all of us just trying to breathe
in a world that doesn't stop for anything.

MY INHERITED RAGE WRITES A POEM

Punch the fucking mirror / watch the shard spear
your ring finger, glisten like a cursed heirloom /
don't honk only once, lean on the horn
until your fist throbs red, until the car wheezes,
breathless / feel me bubbling behind your ribs /
a screaming kettle boiling over, spitting fury
onto raw skin / throwing an axe at a target
won't do / slap yourself across your stupid face / tear out
your hair / bruise your foot on the chair / hurl your phone
across the room / because something has to break
and it can't be you.

THE CLIMB

I haven't climbed a tree in years
but sometimes I stand beneath one,
tilt my head toward the thinnest branches
and trace the path another version
of me might climb.
If only I had the time,
were wearing the right shoes,
could guarantee I won't fall.
I never used to worry
about how I'd get down—
only how the bark bit my palms,
how butterscotch sap kissed the creases
of my fingers together,
how knotted hair stuck
to my sweat-slick neck.
The world always made more sense
from above, and I sometimes wonder
if I might've left
some weightless part of me up there,
long woven into a bowerbird's hoard.
At some point, I decided
to keep my feet on the ground—
learned to think before reaching,
to measure joy like a wing against wind,
to ask if the climb was ever worth
the ache of coming down.

MY GRANDMOTHER IS DEAD AND I'M STANDING IN LINE TO BUY CHICKEN

because what else is there to do but
turn out the rising grief from your pockets
by grocery shopping?
I wonder if the cashier can see on my face
that someone I love is gone.
(And what I really mean is how could he not?)
Four by four by four,
I study the tiles on the floor—
unremarkable squares of beige and gray,
laid out so neatly that I wonder
if they might offer me an answer.
Ridiculous. Almost hateful, really,
how the world keeps spinning,
how the checkout line moves forward,
how there's still dinner to make tonight,
though nothing tastes like it did before.

I DIDN'T KNOW MY GRANDMOTHER WAS A POET

until after she died.
My aunt tells me
she burned every notebook
before she went,
and I picture her striking the match,
flames lighting the deep vault of her eyes
as she watches a lifetime
of words curl in at the edges—
a field after harvest
stripped clean,
the last sheaf gathered,
nothing left for the wind to carry.

A RECURRING DREAM

I am something small
and disoriented—
a pollen-drunk bee tumbling,
leg over wing,
off a hyacinth and straight
into the thrum of wild horses.
I've been here before—
that first flood of panic
crashing through me
like cloudburst in a dry riverbed.
Earth-colored giants blur past,
all thunder and tendon,
manes like smoke,
tails lashing the sky.
Maybe it's the wild Wyoming air,
but I do not settle
into fear like old bones
in an old chair.
Instead, I run.
In this dream,
I know only two things:
I am something small and terrified,
and still, I run wild
as the mustangs
and mares.

YOU WERE TRYING TO GET SOBER

so I took a train to Montana,
watched from my seat as the sun
bruised the sky in pinks and purples.
You met me at the station,
took me straight to the creaky twin bed
in your friend's dad's house
where you couldn't stop hitting
snooze. We got into a fight
when you told me weed didn't count,
and I let your friend believe
it was the backs of *your* shoulders
that struck the closet doors that night.
I wish I could say our story
ended there—that the alarm
finally sounded and I woke up
in a life that wasn't tender to the touch.
But I did not yet know that love
isn't bound to hurt.
I did not yet know that the sun
doesn't color the sky,
but illuminates it.

SADNESS SITS

in my stomach,
has made a home of it
like the spoon
on the dishwasher floor,
its edges softened, worn
by cycle after cycle.
The quiet persistence
of small metal things
is something I've come to admire—
how a stray nail is swallowed by a tree,
how keys outlive the doors they open,
how a penny, turned green, can still be spent,
the way they endure it all,
changed by time and use,
and still manage to catch the light
by its slithering tail,
even if it's just the smallest glint
from the right angle.

CARRY, AS A FEELING

I have yet to bear a heavier
emotion in the scuffed
luggage of my body than
grief. It harbors itself down
deep—a mole, blind to
everything but its own
sorrow, carving heartache
into my ribs like a logger
marking a tree for harvest.

Yesterday, I held grief
between my toes like a
pebble. Today, it is a boulder
that threatens to flatten me
to the dirt. It's all I can do to
eat breakfast, to breathe,
to maintain my life.
To look toward the sun-laced silt
every now and again.
To let the light in.

II

TENDER FLESH

Someone tell me, how is it the clementine
untangles itself so easily? The punch

of a single fingernail and it slips out of its thin
citrus skin like a molting corn snake

or a lickerish lover, giving itself willingly
to the ripened breeze. And tell me, please,

how might I be more like the clementine?
I'd like to shed my battered hull and float

freely with the pappus and the seabirds—
to trust the wind that chooses me and maybe,

eventually, be brave enough to face whatever
tender flesh lies under my own puckered skin.

THE ANGLERFISH

"Rare Deep-Sea Anglerfish Seen for First Time in Broad Daylight"
—*Oceanographic Magazine*, February 10, 2025

We can't know what pulled the anglerfish
up from the darkest waters.

Maybe she was injured,
maybe she got caught in a warm current,
maybe she swallowed a fish with a gas gland,
soaring, like Icarus, too close to the sun.

Or maybe, after a lifetime of shadow,
where survival is quiet and lonely,
she couldn't help but drift
toward the shimmer of something more.

Who are we to decide anything at all
about the little daredevil?

And anyway,
what does it matter?

Sometimes we must let hope
win out over logic—
draw meaning from the depths
because we need to believe that
even at great cost,
there's purpose in the rising.

TOMORROW, MAYBE

It's never more evident to me
that humans are creatures of habit,
of pattern and groove, than when
I'm in the shower and suddenly
become aware that I have washed
my left arm first every day for years—
lather the same path down my legs,
right first, then left. Turn the sponge
to scrub the heels of my feet.
Like a dream hovering over me,
I could draw the map
of this ritual with my eyes closed,
recite it like a prayer from Catholic school.
I wonder what other invisible paths
I've worn into my life—
what other small obediences
were folded into the blueprint
without my knowledge.
I think about the way my mouth
will say yes when my body says no.
Or how I tend to stay too long in rooms
that leave me clinging to the walls
like a cicada shell.
Tomorrow, maybe,
I'll wash my right arm first.
Forget, for a moment,
the paths I thought were mine.
Step into a different room.
Hold the world in both hands
like it's new again,
like I'm new again.

MY FAVORITE ANIMAL IS ME WHEN MY EX-BOYFRIEND'S DAD SAID I WASN'T THE SHARPEST TOOL IN THE SHED

Tool. Like something to be used, toyed with,
broken, replaced / like an insecure man / like
controlled by the hands of another. *Shed*. Like
a snake expanding into thicker skin / like to cast
light or blood or tears or expectations / like she'd
been pared down to nothing. *Sharp*. Like the key
between my knuckles / like the bared cuspids
of a cornered creature / like fingernails whetted into
claws on hateful words / like whittling the dull
softwood of my body sharper and sharper until
you're too afraid to touch.

I DIDN'T CRY THE DAY I FINALLY LEFT YOU

We were lying on your couch,
watching some movie—fast cars,
heroic men—when your hand on my hip
became a wool sweater on bare skin.
I didn't pause the movie,
just shrugged off the itching weight of you,
said it was over,
stood up and gathered my things.
I was shocked when you begged me to stay,
sobbed that you loved me,
that you'd change,
that I was the one.
We both knew you only loved
what you could pin beneath your thumb.
I thought I'd feel relief,
or grief, or anything—
but all I remember
is the screech of tires
as I stepped out the front door,
the life I thought I wanted
now behind me.
On-screen, a man walked away
from a burning building,
never flinching as it collapsed at his back.

WHISPERING LOVE

Everyone wants a love
that sounds like music
blasting, knuckles cracking
jaws, screaming from
rooftops. But what about
a whispering kind of love?
Love quiet as a seed
in soil—gentle like goose
flesh on your neck.
The kind of love you go
still to hear: a heartbeat,
an exhale, a prayer.
Give me a love to eavesdrop
on in a crowded room, like,
Shh, did you hear that?
Can you imagine it?

INVENTORY OF UNNECESSARY APOLOGIES

I'm sorry the house is a mess. Sorry for not
wearing makeup. Sorry for wearing too much
makeup. Sorry it took me a second to put
my wallet back in my purse. Sorry for sending
that landslide of words and sorry also for
following up, dressing silence like an open
wound. Sorry for standing where someone else
wanted to stand. Sorry for laughing loudly.
Sorry for not laughing. Sorry my outfit is cringe.
Sorry for not shaving my legs. Sorry for the razor
burn on my legs. Sorry for breastfeeding in public.
Sorry my baby isn't wearing socks. Sorry my stomach
piles up like dirty laundry when I sit. Sorry
for tearing up at that commercial. Sorry for not replying
to your email while I slept. Sorry for my kid
crying in public. Sorry for giving her my phone
so she stops crying in public. Sorry for not smiling.
Sorry for changing my mind. Sorry for eating
the last slice of pizza. Sorry for not wanting
the last slice of pizza. Sorry for saying sorry.
Sorry for every time I made myself smaller
to make someone else comfortable.

THINGS THAT WERE FOR SURE WRITTEN BY A WOMAN

The way cactus spines guard tender flesh /
and how this is the gilded flicker's preferred
home / the way a bruise blooms in slow
motion / the way wearing red feels like an act
of rebellion / how a key between knuckles
is more prayer than weapon / how laughter
sometimes turns to tears / the way helicopter seeds
dillydally in spirals, resisting the ground
the whole way down / the way grief perches heavy
and aching in your chest like a stray / the tenderness
of moss blanketing stone / the inexplicable urge
to touch something soft / how you can't believe until
you feel it.

LET ME TELL YOU HOW IT FEELS TO BE THIS SOFT

It's like pressing your thumb into room-temp butter
and licking it off / like reading a love poem and feeling
queasy about it / like plugging your ears before the toilet
flushes / like tripping over the shimmer of a slug trail /
like moving the slug off the sidewalk / like too much
peanut butter not enough jelly / like taking one aspirin
when you needed two / like saying a silent sorry
to roadkill / like crying because a kindness caught
you off guard / like crying because a cruelty caught you
off guard / like wearing the wrong pants can't think
of anything else / like sleeping with all your toys so they
don't get sad / like searching every blank face / like do
you like me? / like did I say the wrong thing? / like a dull
ache in your soul / like caring so deeply it splinters your
bones / like why are you so sensitive? / like living with
the volume turned up / like seeing the world sharpened
to a point and holding the lip of it to your collarbone.

MY MOTHER TELLS ME

she hasn't eaten
anything all day
like it's a brag
and not the origin
of my eating disorder.
Her hunger is an
aching animal
after a lifetime
of cowering in the corner.
But even a wolf
born in a cage longs
to sink her teeth
into the moon,
and a woman,
ravenous for life,
can only starve
for so long
before she devours
everything in sight.

FIRST IMPRESSIONS

I overheard a woman
on a first date say
her body is really
just a soft vehicle
to carry her brain.

A gondola without
a gondolier is only
a chunk of wood,
and this body
is the least interesting
thing about me.

A mush of
mud and sticks
not meant for you
or for them,
but for sightseeing
this terrible and
wonderful world.

I AM EATING A HANDFUL OF FIGS

and I think about how I can't eat a fig
without also eating a fig wasp.
I pinch each swollen bell in two,
autopsy the punch-berry guts
for wings or antennae
or a black and amber ghost.
I do this—live my life like I might
bite into a stinger.
Better safe than sorry,
I hear myself saying.
But the thing about figs
is they aren't meant
to be eaten cautiously—
so worried about the potential yuck
you never taste the sweetness.
This, too, is how I've approached
so many of life's sweetnesses:
splitting them open to inspect for loss
before letting the juice touch my tongue.
It's not that I want to be afraid—
only that I've spent so long
bracing for sorrow
I've forgotten how to recognize joy.
Still, I want to trust the fruit.
I want to eat the whole fig,
wasp and all.

BREAKING FORMATION

Every morning
and every evening,
a line of pelicans
snakes a ride
on a warm wind,
skates the shoreline,
wings barely moving,
as if they were born
knowing this path—
something handed down
without explanation.
Sometimes I'll see one break formation,
drift a little higher
than the others,
catch a rebellious current
and, for the length
of a held breath,
forget its rank,
remember
the endless sky.

THE DOGWOOD

It's early June and every morning
the dogwood,
a cumulus of fluffy white flowers
outside my bedroom window,
fools me into thinking it has snowed.
Funny, how the mind's branches
bend toward what it knows—
sees piles of white and thinks winter,
hears silence and thinks absence.
How happiness,
if it arrives too gently—
weightless as a hummingbird
perched on the spire of the world—
can feel like a sleight of heart.

HUMANS ARE THE ONLY SPECIES KNOWN TO BLUSH

Despite the great lengths we pace
to appear calm and composed,
our thin skins of need betray us
in tenderness,
as if the plague of apathy
never reached the blood,
as if the mutinous emotions
simmering beneath the surface
can't help but revolt against
the guarding of the heart,
a flare of vulnerability
shot straight through the shell
like a warning
or a prayer—
a rose flush of *I'm still here,*
a chest rush of *I care, I care.*

ZOMBIE SALMON

For twenty-nine
years I was
a writer
who did
not write,
which is a lot
like when
a salmon
begins to rot
before they die—
what's left,
then, when
you start
losing pieces
of yourself to
the whitewater
current of
the world,
except to start
swimming
like your brief
and wondrous
life depends
on it?

A BROKEN RULE

I learned that people were never meant to see their own faces
and now every mirror feels like a broken rule,
a door swung open to a room I was never supposed to enter.
The thing is, a swallow does not glimpse herself
mid-flight and spend the rest of the day smoothing her feathers
or questioning the grace of her swoop,
and I was never meant to witness
the curve of dark brown pores that frame my aquiline nose,
or the precise way my mouth folds around a name.
What good does it do me to see that my features
are not perfectly symmetrical? I have memorized myself
too well, learned my face more intimately
than my mother's, my sister's, my lover's,
when I was only supposed to see my own eyes
reflected back through shining pond water—
existing in motion, in laughter, in breath,
then vanishing from myself the moment
a fish breaks the surface, swallowing
my vanity whole before I drown in it.

IN ANOTHER LIFE, I AM KIND TO MY BODY

In another life,
maybe in my next life,
my body is not a holding cell
for man's morality, not heavy
with the grief of what it is
and what it has never been.
My skin is just skin.
My fat, only fat.
I let this body ripen past green,
graze the splits and russets
with the backs of my fingers.
I dress it in tomato red,
unafraid to be seen,
to jostle for space.
In this life, joy drips
sweet and sticky
from my elbows,
and I lick it off,
unashamed.
Oh, how good
it will taste,
all that space.

TO THE WOMAN AT THE PATISSERIE WHO TURNED DOWN CAKE BECAUSE SHE WAS "TRYING TO BE GOOD"

After Kim Addonizio

If you ever counted calories like sins ever
skipped breakfast to deserve dinner turned
down a slice only to binge a pint in the dim
light of the fridge opened your throat
to the toilet bowl received a compliment
like holy communion called hunger discipline
brought your own meal to a dinner party ordered
a salad when you wanted the steak told yourself
nothing tastes as good as skinny feels swallowed
the ache with a glass of warm lemon water
/ listen that was never goodness / listen
you were always already good.

THE THINGS WE LEAVE BEHIND

There is a ledger tucked between my collarbones,
where I've tallied the debts I never agreed to.
My mother's temper *(check),*
my grandma's grief *(check),*
her mother's indifference *(check).*
Us women are burial grounds.
Our wombs carry heirlooms, cardinal red
and heavy as hell, left to us by the women
before, and before, and before.

I sift through the ledger—some debts I pay,
others are ash on my tongue.
No doubt, I'll add new dues for my own
daughter, who one day will trace these lines.
And, like my mother and her mother,
my hope for my daughter
is that she might just burn it all,
scatter it without ceremony
across some empty parking lot,
no traces left behind.

GENERATIONAL HEALING

I hung a drawing of a naked woman
in my daughter's room,
her earthy form framed by blackberries,
wildflowers, and the moon.
Every night, as I rock my baby,
feed her from my breast,
I study the woman's hips
wide as a promise, her belly
open as a meadow, her body
whole and relaxed and true.
Every night, I stare at this woman,
commit her to memory.
I think to myself,
Isn't she beautiful?
This is what I want for my daughter—
a life untouched by shame,
a body untouched by expectation.
I hung a drawing of a naked woman
in my daughter's room,
but it was never for her.
I was the one who needed to learn
how to look at softness
and call it beautiful,
how to witness a body being
full, present, unworried.
To exist inside my own skin
as gently as I want my daughter to.

IN THE BATH

my one-and-a-half-year-old daughter
pours water into my cupped palms.
She watches in wonder
as a soapy universe swirls
in the same hands that carry her.
On the other side of the door,
where the world is rusting
from the inside out,
my hands are useless as slugs.
I squeeze my fingers tight,
desperate to hold on
to this tender magic
for a little while longer.

MY SISTER

When she was small,
my sister believed
the moon was hers—
a soft-eyed friend who floated
behind us on late-night drives,
whose familiar face,
bright as baby teeth,
shone through her window
as she fell asleep.
In childhood, hope
isn't something you learn,
it simply waits for you,
constant and glowing
as a porch light,
tagging itself along to school,
to soccer, to visit your dad in another state—
a witness to your greatest loves
and greater losses,
waiting just outside the door,
ready to follow you anywhere.
I hope she knows the moon is still hers.
I hope I hope I hope.

I PAID AN ETSY WITCH $14.86 FOR BETTER LUCK

In other words, the only thing I know for certain
is that I don't know shit.
I was tired of the way things were going—
bad luck and blackberry thorns
snagging my wrists on every sidewalk.
So I purchased a prayer via PayPal—
paid a stranger in a velvet profile picture
to rearrange my stars for the cost of lunch.
I was willing to be whimsical, if a bit foolish,
if it meant I could keep hope in my palm.
And anyway, who is it that decides what's real?
Every atom in me was once inside a star,
and it's only because the earth leans a little
that bare branches give way to blossoms.
Tell me that isn't magic.
I wanted to believe
in anything that kept me believing.
Tell me hope isn't the oldest spell we know.

UNEXPECTED SHORES

I am not someone who waits
for the water to still,
for the cake to cool,
for the persimmon to soften.

I have never been one
to smooth the surface,
to let the current choose
its direction before

rushing headlong into it—
unfurling sails in storms,
eating cake while the frosting runs,
biting into fruit too firm.

Impatience has built me
a house of unfurnished rooms,
peppered my pockets with loose pearls,
left me breathless from

pacing the ache that always runs ahead.
And yet, it's led me to unexpected shores,
where the horizon is within reach
if only you dare wade into the deep.

III

AFTER THE FIRE, WILDFLOWERS

The first thing back
was the smell of coffee,
then the sound of the heater
clicking on like a throat
clearing before a song.
I didn't want to want anything.
But I started to notice the sun—
how it spilled across the floor,
light as champagne,
sticky as grief.
I've been here before.
This is how these things go.
There's no moment,
no music swelling
or trumpet of return,
just days that keep arriving,
and me,
continuing to meet them
before I fully know how.

EVEN HERE

I watch from the corner chair
as you kiss your grandma's forehead,
your thumb stroking her hairline
with a tenderness that stings my eyes;
watch as you remind her of all the times
she played catch with you in the Seattle rain,
how much those wet afternoons meant,
how you'll do the same with your kids;
watch as you press your cheek to hers,
whispering *I love you*s and *thank you*s;
watch the way your eyelashes flicker
like candlewicks in a gentle wind
when you don't know what to say,
when you study her face each time
she closes her eyes; and I understand,
seeing love laid bare like this, spread across
the room like all those Christmas dinners
crammed into her basement—
folding tables end to end,
mismatched tablecloths from years past—
that sorrow this full is only possible
because love made a home there first,
passed from hand to hand like a warm plate.
How even here, it keeps feeding us.

"WE GRIEVE IN ACCORDANCE WITH HOW MUCH WE LOVE"

is what the mortician says
when I ask her about grief.
It's grief that sloshes
in my stomach, sticks
sap-like to my skin,
settles fine as dust
in my bones.
I will never know a life
without grief.
Loving you is a golden
thread woven into
the brocade of me—
one pull and the whole
thing unravels.

THINGS THAT WERE FOR SURE WRITTEN BY A MOTHER

The way spit-up stains flower into Rorschach tests
on every shirt / like what does it mean? /
like will we be okay?? / the way pink mold blooms
lazy around the drain / the pull of tiny fingers
curled like question marks / the patient ache
of rocking a baby back to sleep / back to sleep /
please, back to sleep / the way a mother's breath
smells of grief and joy / devotion and longing /
how her heart blisters with unraveling / the puckered
skin beneath sore to the touch / a tenderness exposed
from giving so much / being so much.

A MOTHER'S ALPHABET

And all at once, you are everything,
Balance teetering between bliss and burnout.
Crying (all of us, crying!) in the Cimmerian night.
Drenched in darkness,
Every moment feels endless.
Fingers sticky with fascination, frustration,
Gratitude, grief. Growing pains in your
Hollowed-out hands, holding on to hope like an
Injured bird on the ice—
Just trying to juggle it all, to *enjoy it while it lasts*, to
Keep from crumbling.
Longing in the low light for a life long-gone until
Morning slips in, mild and merciful, and you're made
New from nap and need and newborn breath.
One foot in front of the other, you
Pick up pacifiers, prenatals, pieces of yourself.
Quiet moments rest calmly on your chest,
Remind you there is rhythm to be found in
Small joys—soft skin, sleepy sighs, seeing
Tiny half-moon fingers
Unfurl like an Ursinia flower—
Validating every sleepless night, every
Worried whisper, wishing you could
Xerox each unextraordinary moment into your cortex.
You carry all of it, holy as yellow yolk,
Zipping the jagged edges of the rising sun whole again.

SAVAGE

I was forty weeks and three days pregnant, belly bursting, everything
hanging heavy like an overripe plum on its bowstring branch.

My husband used the word *savage*, watching me claw and heave

my way through the forty-eight-hour labor, the drug-free birth
of our daughter, and I have to agree: I'd never felt more animal,

more ancient. They say you forget—the only reason you do it again—

but I remember every breathless detail. I remember the way my baby
fluttered her feet inside my deflating belly, a farewell kick before the final

tearing push that would split me open and cleave us from one into two.

How in the thick smoke of pain I turned away from faces, from voices,
driven down, inward, until I was looking up at myself from some well

in the deepest part of me. But most of all, I remember the scooped-out

hollowness of my freshly emptied womb—how it howled inside me
like a raw, aching wind, mourning even as it rejoiced. How terrifying

and thrilling that I now held in my arms such a vulnerable piece of myself.

A nerve, exposed. That's what's savage, I think: to love something
so fiercely, knowing the world will not spare it—

learning to live with your heart beating helplessly outside your body.

BEING A MOTHER IS

touching someone else's poop before you've had your morning coffee / waving at every squirrel / sloppy open-mouth baby kisses / pausing the movie / pausing sex / pausing everything to soothe the baby / wishing they'd stay this small forever / wishing you could reason with them / feeling like your heart lives outside your body / listening to "The Happy Song" until it rings in your ears / trying to be present / knowing that you're living in the good old days / picking fuzzies out of sticky toes / scream-crying into your tired palms / baby breath you wish you could bottle / bitten and bleeding breasts / little eyes searching for yours / being desperate for a break / being desperate to hold them close / overwhelming / life-affirming / terrifying / gratifying / exhausting / absolutely everything.

WEAK SPOTS

are what the dentist calls
the yellowing edges
of my daughter's eyeteeth,
reaching two gloved thumbs
into the pockets of her cheeks,
pulling her lips up and back,
revealing a failure that bites
through my heart's thin skin.
Weak spots, she says again,
tapping the fuzzed borders
where tooth meets gum,
where care was clearly
worn a bit thin.
I want to defend myself—
to convince the dentist
I'm not a bad mother,
explain that my baby
got her teeth at three months,
how between bitten breasts
and baby-led weaning,
I could barely keep up
with the unrelenting list
of things good mothers do,
all of it sticky and stacking up
like plaque—far enough
beneath the lip to let slip.
I want to tell her
how the quiet,
unrelenting panic that
I'm doing everything wrong
keeps me up at night.

Did I remember to tend to
the weak spots?
Did I do enough today?
Was I enough today?
And the true answer
is sometimes I don't,
I didn't, I wasn't.
Motherhood, I've learned,
is a series of soft failures,
survived with love.
I ask myself again and again:
Isn't she still laughing?
Isn't her smile still full?

EVERY DAY, PREEMPTIVELY

The day before her second birthday,
my daughter tells me she misses me.
Standing, potbelly clad in her bubble bath,
suds sliding down her baby doll legs,
she says, for the first time,
"I. miss. you. Mama."
I'd just been holding her moments ago,
but even the smallest distance
was enough to create that ache—
the one that feels like hands pressed
on either side of a glass door.
I lean down and kiss her wet hair,
let her soapy arms soak the collar of my shirt.
I don't know how to tell her
that I miss her every day, preemptively.
I miss the baby she was,
the toddler she is,
the self she's steadily outgrowing.
I hold her like water,
watch each moment drip from my hands,
knowing I'll spend my whole life
learning to let her go.

TOLERABLE DISTANCE

Don't leave me ever again, not even to the grocery store.

You are falling asleep in my arms
for the first time in months,
weepy from a hot August day
and a skipped nap.
Suddenly, you need me close
in the same way I need you close—
my nose in your hair, your cheek
to my chest, our arms like ropes.
If I do my job right, each day
the space where I end and you begin
widens, the tolerable distance
growing as you do,
farther than my arms can reach,
at a pace my heart can't match,
all the way to the grocery store
and then some.

TWO SIDES OF THE SAME MOON

After Pink Floyd

The day I told my family about my pregnancy
was the same day my sister lost hers.
Fourteen weeks along and none of us knew
a second pulse birled beneath her skin.
The nurse couldn't give a reason.
Sometimes a note unspools into a melody,
sometimes it splits mid-
measure.

The space between us was a prism—
shattered light scattering,
shards caught in the weave of carpet,
joy bleeding into sorrow,
sorrow bending into joy.

Two sides of the same moon,
like that photo of us when we were kids,
pressed back to back, elbows linked
into a constellation we never named,
blurring the cloud-covered yard
into a kaleidoscope, quickening
every color into one.

The only thing we knew then,
and the only thing we know still,
is that it all keeps on spinning and
spinning—the song ends where it began,
the suncatcher is restless on its hook,
and the turning moon carves
its certain path across the sky.

GRIEF SALAD

Instructions:

1. Gather your grief from the garden—fresh is best, but dried will do.

2. Place in a velvet-lined bowl. Set it on your tallest shelf and let yourself forget about it for a while.

3. When you're ready, set your oven to *fucking scorching* and sharpen your knife on your teeth.

4. Once your blood cools, promise God you'll do better through chopped sobs and salted tears.

5. Work the grief gently with your hands. Stretch and fold until smooth.
Note: Grief is heavy. If your arms get tired, set it down and rest.

6. Go back and repeat steps 2–5 periodically and randomly, as needed.

7. Eventually—slowly—it'll start to take the form of hope. If it looks more like tolerance, that's okay too.
Note: This recipe is hard to follow and doesn't make much sense.

8. Plate on your good china and serve with a side of self-compassion. Garnish with a sprinkle of joy (optional).

9. Enjoy next to a bright window with a cup of *keep going* in your favorite mug.

10. Wrap leftovers in mourning silks and store in your front pocket.
Note: There's a good chance you'll be eating grief salad for a while, so please adjust recipe to your own tastes.

MIGHT SHOULD

My grandmother was the only person
I've ever heard use the phrase *might should*—
the uncommon marriage of two helping verbs
that, when joined, suggest both
hesitation and intent.
To be brave and unsure,
to hold two contradicting things
in the same mouth.
It was a weld of words that, to my child brain,
meant almost nothing,
like a middle name or a silent *e*.
I might should call her back.
We might should go to the grocery store.
You might should bring a jacket.

After she died, the phrase swirled
and sloshed through my brain—
pulled me into the undertow, where her voice
now exists as a shell song.
My grandmother was a woman who
placed her words like stepping-stones:
thoughtfully, deliberately.

All these years later, I understand why,
of the phrases she might have favored,
she chose the one that sounded
like the hush between tides—
one that left a bit of space
for pause, for grace, for things still taking shape.

STONES BENEATH THE SAND

While walking the beach,
I heard an old man say to his friend,
I mean, I'm still grieving over
my high school sweetheart.
It wasn't a confession,
but a fact—clear as the waves
are restless, breaking like breath.
His friend didn't answer right away,
simply nodded, like *of course,*
of course some things stay
and settle deep,
stones beneath the sand
that shape the shore.
Meanwhile, the ocean folds itself
over like an endless blanket,
clearing the strand,
then bringing it all back.

MY GRANDMA WAS A GIRL

when she became someone's mother.
Just seventeen—
still soft in the face, still someone's baby.
Childhood clung to her
like the last light before dusk.

I was twenty-nine
when I first held my girl.
Old enough to have painted
the nursery Shoji White,
to grieve the life that would split
like a dropped pear when she came.
Even then, I wasn't ready.

Even when you choose motherhood,
when you walk toward it with open hands,
knowing it'll take your wallet and your watch,
you still feel robbed.

It's a kind of giving
that doesn't look like a gift
until further up the hill.

My God, I never understood until now:
She lost so much / She left us with so much.

I WAS RAISED IN A HOUSE OF WOMEN

Women whose laughter cracked like thunder—
scared the shivering dogs on the couch;
women who fought messy and relentless
as the foaming tide—who'd drag you
into the rip current
then guide you back to shore;
women who'd pop the zits you couldn't reach,
whose loose hair clogged every drain—
pulled from the pipes, long and dark,
like something unnamable,
untamable; women
who carried grief in with the groceries,
who'd call you *bub* and tell you
normal is boring, anyway.

I FED MY DAUGHTER FROM MY BREAST

for two and a half holy years.
Through teething and fevers,
long days and longer nights,
she tethered to me
the same way a prayer might
in the most desperate hours,
the kind that breathes warm
hope against your skin,
that presses closer
as the dark draws in.
I gave her everything I had—
the tea I reheated and never drank,
my sleep in stolen handfuls,
the only body I'll ever get—
and yes, my nipples now
point at unfamiliar angles,
and yes, I live in a body
that doesn't yet remember
how not to be needed,
but just listen
to the way she laughs,
look how she carries it all
in the pinks of her cheeks—
a girl stitched
from the very fabric of myself,
wearing my love like a birthright.

MY DAUGHTER WON'T REMEMBER

how the crooks of my elbows held her
in the weeping morning light; how I'd whisper
"you're okay, we're okay" like the desperate
prayer it was; how I'd hum Norah Jones until
my throat tasted like moonlight; how I'd study
the candlelit flutter at the crown of her head;
how I'd kiss the budding soles of her feet
before zipping her pajamas; how the metronome
creak of the secondhand rocking chair lulled
us both to sleep; how when she'd ask for a story
in the darkest hours of the night, I'd recite
Goodnight Moon from memory; how I'll know
it all by heart for the rest of my days.

GENERATIONAL HEALING II

I'm shocked when my daughter
points to the drawing
above her changing table—
the woman, bare and at ease,
her form curved like a riverbend,
soft as a lullaby—
and calls it *Mama*.

Just like that,
the body I have spent years
apologizing for,
sucking in, smoothing down,
becomes bigger
than how small it can be—
no longer a before or after,
no longer a question to be answered.

My daughter doesn't see
the years I spent trying to be less,
or the doubt that lives in me
like a crooked spine.
She sees no flaw, no failure,
only the body that carries her,
carries me.

I'M BAD AT TAKING CARE OF PLANTS

My mother's thumb is green
as April, but mine hovers somewhere
around February—unsure,
too much, then not enough.
Under my care, the soil
is either drowning or dust-dry,
root rot or cracked crust.
I never get it quite right.

I tend to joy with the same
unsteady hands:
smothering it with wanting,
then leaving it to wilt in the dark,
unsure when to prune it,
when to leave it be.

And yet, somehow,
a thin stem will push through.
A new leaf will emerge,
thin and stubborn,
reaching for the light,
determined to unfurl despite
the uncertain mess of it all.

STRAY BONES

If I closed my eyes and walked,
one calloused foot in front of the other,
would I make it to your door?
Or slip into circles,
like green eyes coiled in gold?
Optimistic little creatures, humans,
believing we can thread a straight path
through a forest that aches to keep us.
Haven't I stepped over that same branch?
Didn't I grieve at that grave before?
No beacon, no mountain, no star—
and still, we go on,
willing to misplace ourselves,
to let our stray bones off-leash,
hoping they remember
the way back.

WILD INDULGENCE

There is a woman in my neighborhood
with not one, but six
full-grown St. Bernard dogs.
She tethers them to her waist
and trots the happy troop
up and down the street.
I see her and think *What a wild indulgence*,
to gather so much joy it orbits you
in a glorious parade of gluttony,
as if she leaves the house and dares
the world to question
how much happiness one person deserves.
It's ridiculous, of course—
but so is happiness,
so is the heart's hunger
for more and more and more.

I TOLD HIM

I didn't want anything serious,
not after the last boy
beat my heart black and blue.
I had a habit of avoiding
anything gentle,
anything that felt like
a room with the door left open.
My grandma told me
to give him a chance,
like she'd watched me
walk past spring
with my coat still buttoned.
Sometimes I think about
how close I came
to unlacing the future—
a dream where you miss your train
and wake with an aching throat
as if someone else
cried in your skin.

MORSE CODE

Sometimes when
you hold me close,
cheek to chest,
the pads of my
fingers echo your
heartbeat in reflex—
tap-tap, onto your
back in Morse code:
tap-tap *I love-love*
you. Tap-tap *I need*
you, like, scary. Tap-tap
I wear your heart
on my sleeve. Tap-tap
until our bones brittle.

BOWING CRANES

We didn't dance
at our courthouse wedding—
always more bowing cranes
than mayflies rising—
and when the day was over,
when we were too tired
to take our bodies to bed,
we stayed tangled on the couch,
my toes pressed into your calves—
a night not of fire, but ember,
building something to warm our
palms when the season turns,
as it always does,
and I still think back to junior year
when my English teacher asked the class
if anyone had ever been in love,
and I was the only one
to raise my hand,
and how he looked at me and laughed—
said, *Picture him on the toilet,*
a crying baby in your arms,
then tell me you're in love.
And sure, we were only kids,
fumbling clumsy fingers over the wet
clay of ourselves, of each other,
but now, a decade later,
I know all your bedroom moves by heart,
and you got the towel when I pissed myself
during labor, and just yesterday
I took a photo of you on the toilet,
our daughter beside you

on her tiny training potty,
all of us laughing,
love stretched but not torn,
tired hands still raised and reaching,
two bodies bending toward each other
again and again in the shallows.

I JOINED A CLOUD APPRECIATION GROUP ON FACEBOOK

because the great hurts
tend to be universal,
but so is marveling at the sky.
It's easy to get lost scrolling
a digital cloudscape
where (per the group rules)
there is no discussion of
politics / religion / conspiracy / astrology /
climate change / MLMs / children / aliens—
and so we speak only
in the language of clouds:
the fleeting cirrus clouds in Western Cape,
the way nimbostratus clouds hang
heavy and dark and impossibly low,
how all of us (all of us!)
are still looking up.

JOY IS COMING

After Kim Addonizio

but it's a train that never
hits its scheduled hour.
It's tangled in traffic,
snagged on barbed wire,
held up by weather,
wandering through
the wrong neighborhood,
stopping to browse
every Little Free Library.
I worry it's gone for good this time,
but then it appears in a flicker—
a goldfinch in the corner of my eye,
the muted G-major strum
of "Banana Pancakes,"
a familiar perfume trailing off
a stranger's coat, gone
just before I can place it.
Joy is coming, I know it is—
it's right around the corner,
showing up like an old friend,
swinging open the back door
like it never left,
unannounced and unhurried,
hands full of flowers
it picked along the way,
a little late but somehow
right on time.

IV

I DO NOT ORDER TWO RAW SUGARS IN MY AMERICANO

But the barista at my local spot
doesn't know that. Or she doesn't care.
I've tried to tell her,
but she sees my face and laces my cup
like a grandmother
who won't take no for an answer.
Despite myself, I soften into this small insistence.
Did you know a black coffee
has just two calories?
Add cream and it swells to forty-two.
Sugar, and it surges another hundred.
This information matters only when
the size of your body is more important
than the size of your joy.
Yet, even when we don't ask for it,
even when we insist against it,
joy always finds us again.
One day soon it will sweeten your coffee,
or curl into the crook of your elbow,
or nest in your magnolia,
and you'll say, *Yes, yes, I remember.*

THE ONE WHERE I CONFESS THAT I CAN'T DO IT ALL

Or rather, I do not want to.
When my dad asks me if I've been busy,
I tell him no. As a girl, I was told
over and over that I can (should!)
do it all, have it all, be it all.
I was still in my training bra when I realized
I want to live a life with legroom. I want
to sojourn deliciously like sun tea in Florida heat.
I want to sip it in the garden so slowly
it grays in my cup. I want to read three books
at a time, none of them personal development.
I want the smell of sunshine and grass
to perfume my skin—to be made of salt
and lichen and mud instead of spreadsheet
and status and productivity. I want to live
at the pattering pace of my nervous system.
I do not want to spend my one precious life
doing and having and being everything,
only to enjoy nothing.

YOU ARE A SONGBIRD

The secret is:
You can live as many lives
as the brown thrasher has songs,
each one flaring bright
as copper in the sun.
Imagine telling the brown thrasher
she had only one song to sing
when her heart knew thousands—
how she might have folded
her bright hunger
into something small and quiet,
might never have discovered
she is a songbird at all.
What a loss for the world:
the air missing something
it was meant to carry,
the trees aching with silence,
if the brown thrasher
never found her voice.

SMALL INCONVENIENCES

Anthony Bourdain once said
if you're too lazy to peel garlic,
you don't deserve to eat it,
which I take to mean:
In a pre-minced world,
where everyone searches
for meaning in mediocrity,
where we're too quick to dismiss
the quiet scrape of a knife,
the hiss of cloves in hot butter,
a sliver of time
golden at the edges,
please bother with an existence
that is slow-simmered, sticky-fingered,
full of the big flavors
and small inconveniences
that make up a life.

OROGENESIS

I forgot
to buy paper
plates, so dishes
pile in the sink, one
on top of another on
top of another, sliding
and colliding, a convergence
of all our busy lives. The night
grows longer and the mountain taller,
evidence that we are too together to worry about
the mess, just as we should be, if only for a few hours.

WHO AM I WHEN THE LIGHTS GO OUT?

I am all the books I've pressed
to the tender spot in my chest.
I am the slug of beeswax,
paused mid-candle.
I am the cat bones long buried
in the backyard,
and every page I tore
from my own journal.
I am the whisper of Chanel No. 5
on my shoulder,
the fingertip taste of clover honey,
the color blue,
the verdant breath of cut grass,
the Sacagawea dollar
tucked in my overalls pocket.
I am every time I stitched
my heart back together,
needling through scar tissue and char.
In the dark,
I palm the worn corners,
the sharp edges,
everything that made me.
And despite it all,
I do not vanish
when the filament blinks off.

LET ME TELL YOU HOW A STITCH ONLY SNAPS WHEN IT'S WORN TOO THIN

I haven't been to yoga in months,
broke my gua sha in the sink,
didn't eat enough protein today,
forgot to take my vitamins.
Most days, I don't drink water
until noon. Warm lemon water? Never.
Coffee with cream and two raw sugars, please.
I do not meditate. Rarely journal.
I have sworn off ice baths and fasting
and gluten-free baking, and my god,
I have never been more well.
For so long my skin hung threadbare
from my bones—
stretched to fit any shape
but my own, mending invented holes
until my fingers bled, hands too full
of frayed edges to raise a fist.
I've learned that a woman
who wears herself unaltered
is not perfect, but free:
the loose thread
that may just unravel it all.

I AM SOFTER NOW,

shaped and smoothed
by what passed through me—
a riverbed after a flood.
A body that has carried life
becomes something new,
something endless,
remade by time and touch.
It knows how to cradle
the crying current,
how to bend and curve
into whatever form
is needed of it—
a willingness to be
only what it needs to be
is what carries it forward,
carries us all forward.

CHEEKS

I spent years wishing away my cheeks,
prayed to a god I didn't believe in
to give my body the elegance of hunger—
something less like a ripe pear,
more like its core, stripped to seed.
Please, make me narrow as a reed,
unburdened by bloom and blush.
Now, my daughter smiles at me
with those same cheeks,
round as a question, perfect as a peony,
soft and sure, untouched by *too much*.
And what is fullness, if not bounty?
The sugar-swell of ripe fruit,
fields heavy with grain,
branches thick with blossom,
rivers brimming with rain.
We praise abundance in everything—
what spills over, what thrives beyond need,
what rises and stretches toward the sun.
Everything except the bodies of women.
Again, I pray to a god I don't believe in:
Let our cheeks be too full
of joy, of bread, of breath
to utter an apology for them.
Let no one name
beautiful abundance a flaw.

MAYBE YOU'RE NOT PRETTY. SO WHAT?

After @horriblemeanbadwoman

Maybe you're too busy being something else,
something better. Someone who holds words
in your mouth like cherry stones, spits them sharp
across the yard. Someone who names things—
who knows the difference between a sparrow
and a swallow, between being seen and being
known. Someone who has laughed so hard
you forgot yourself, who shouts into train tunnels
just to hear your own voice, big and bouncing.
Someone who does not wait for the sky to open
before believing. Someone who has run barefoot,
smelling of grass and sweat, who has swallowed
joy in breathless gasps, who knows that pretty
has never built a fire, never written a novel,
never started a revolution.

WHAT I MEAN WHEN I SAY I'M AN IMPERFECT WOMAN

I do not stretch after I work out. Sometimes,
I do not work out and instead let the rind
of my body compost into my couch.
I do not want sex every night. Or every week.
Despite my best efforts, I still do not care
about sports. Despite my best efforts, I still think
the word *bitch*. My face is not symmetrical.
Neither are my breasts. I do not read Tolstoy or
Shakespeare or Brontë—I prefer books
you'd keep facedown at a family dinner.
I rarely clean the toilet. Or refill the paper towels.
Or text back. When a man makes me
uncomfortable, I am often the one apologizing.
No matter how cute I feel, a bad photo
will always ruin my mood. My legs, bruised
like plantains. My heart, pliant as an overripe
peach, thumbs plunged pit-deep. I am a dark
cave, a restless waterfall, an impulsive hot spring—
a glorious blemish on the earth's crust.

WHAT I MEAN WHEN I SAY I'M AN IMPERFECT MOTHER

I do not fold her clothes into drawers, or pair
her tiny socks, or remember to rotate her toys.
I do not want to get on my hands and knees
and be a kitty, or serve stuffed animals tea,
or play check-up for the hundredth time.
Sometimes, I tell her *Just a second* and scroll
longer than I mean to. I have set her down
at the baby gate and screamed my rage into
a pile of laundry. I forget things: the extra diaper,
the sunscreen, how fast she's growing. I let her
eat in the car. I let her wear pajamas to the store.
I say no when I could say yes. I long for silence,
then miss her voice the moment she falls asleep.
I am the floor my daughter spills her life across,
not polished or spotless, but unmovable beneath her.
Then again, she has never asked me for gleaming
perfection—only to hold her, only to show up again
and again and again.

MY DAUGHTER

came from an egg
no bigger than the head of a pin
that lived inside my body
since before I was born.
My mother carried the two of us,
my grandma carried the three of us,
and on and on and on.
That's the thing about women—
even through the cruelest winds
we hold each other like this,
a flame behind a cupped palm,
hope like a twitching canary
in the hollows of our wombs,
keeping ourselves alight.

I AM EXACTLY LIKE OTHER GIRLS

A paper doll cut from the same
pre-teen magazine, creased
in all the same places
from folding ourselves smaller
and smaller.

But paper folded enough times
becomes impossible to tear,
and stacked,
each layer presses back
unyielding as steel—
becomes something
unbreakable
in its togetherness.

IN THIS POEM, I WILL PROVE I AM NOT WHO I WAS

I dance at weddings now.
I compliment people instead of
quartering jealousy. I don't dream
about being trampled by horses.
I let go and go and go. I triple-fold
my towels. I order dessert even if
I'm the only one. I'm not afraid
of being a little cringe. I've stopped
checking Goodreads before I pick
up a new book. I've started wearing
colors again (pink and blue and
even sometimes red)! I tell people I
love them. And I let myself love them.
I wear my natural curls. I'm no longer
a candle in the wind—I'm a blackbird
riding the windy treetops and when I slip,
I just spread my wings and soar.

I WILL BE FORGOING HOT GIRL SUMMER IN EXCHANGE FOR

crusty baguette and triple-cream brie girl
summer / dirt moons under my nails / iced
coffee in a jam jar / yes only when I mean it
girl summer / too much flaky salt / toast
thick as my wrist girl summer / kiss my baby
in the garden / rosemary prayer between
my palms / let the email sit girl summer /
paperback in my purse / watch the jasmine
claim the house / splitting fat figs on my tongue
girl summer / thighs stuck to the lawn chair /
basil tops / peachsoft / deep breath / no bra
girl summer / dishes can wait / ugly with
joy girl summer / hips ripened on the vine
girl summer / settle into the body
that is mine girl summer.

IT'S ALWAYS THE SAME THINGS THAT GET ME

Dark chocolate, red wine, salted butter,
sourdough bread, a stained recipe card,
cinnamon lip balm, a dab of blush on the nose,
an afternoon freed up, fingers laced across
a table, a small country of gentleness,
the blue breath of night at the window,
a thin seam of light under the door,
my daughter's cheek pressed to my chest—
the soft weight of her head holding me here.

YOU DO NOT HAVE TO

After Mary Oliver

leave your city, your job, your life and *eat,*
pray, love yourself into oblivion to be happy.
You do not have to burn it all to the ground
and bossbitch, exodus, manifest your way
into a life worth living. You only have to let
the swell of what is most true spill from you
not as a tsunami, but a bayou: a slow-moving
arrival, poorly defined yet lush with soul.

THE FIRST SIGN OF CIVILIZATION

You might think, as I did,
that the first sign of civilization
was the wheel, or harnessed fire,
or sharpened stone, or cave walls
stenciled with ochre hands.
But it was a healed bone—
a femur, broken clean through
and mended back to bearing weight.
Here's the thing: A break like that
in the wild is a death sentence.
Ask any fox or fawn
if they've survived a broken leg.
If you can't walk, you don't eat.
If you don't run, you can't survive.
Nature is ruthless, indifferent, unforgiving.
But we humans have a capacity
for compassion that interrupts instinct,
that rewrites the script of survival—
a tenderness so crucial to who we are
that we etched our origin not in stone,
but in mercy, in kindness.

THE NEWS IS HEAVY

After Ellen Bass

but did you hear the musk ox at the zoo
had a baby? And the aurora borealis danced
in spring Alabama skies? Last week, a mother
of five made a dress entirely of fresh dahlias,
and don't you think if joy had a closet
that's exactly what she would wear? I once
heard a woman say she was saved by an injured
chicken. Isn't that the most wonderfully
human thing you've ever heard? Think,
for a heartbeat or two, of every great thing:
sleeping with the windows open, the burble
of the coffeepot, a vine-ripened cherry
tomato, sun-warmed goosebump skin
out from the cover of shade, pealing bells
in the distance—this is where hope lives.

MY HUSBAND CRIES

when he reads the poems I write
about our daughter.
He clears his throat—
winks a teary joke
about onions or allergies,
tells me how he didn't know
there were words for that feeling
until now,
and in the way he looks at me,
the way he looks at our girl,
I hear the poem
reading itself back.

SALAD FOR DINNER

After Danusha Laméris

I tell you I love you,
but it's salad for dinner.
Doesn't scratch the itch,
doesn't quell the hunger,
only moves the ache from my stomach
to my throat,
makes the wanting unbearable—
a word on the tip of the tongue,
a match that won't catch.
What I mean is I want
to fuse the webs of our fingers
together, sticky as burnt sugar—
move through the world
like a tongue chasing honey,
a braid of dragonflies,
two struck tuning forks,
frantic and unbound
from their immutable bodies.
My teeth want to scrape
the salted bone of you clean,
split your pomegranate mouth
and chew the seeds.
My lungs want to asphyxiate
on your out-breath—
full to the brim with nothing but you.

DEVOUR YOUR NICE THINGS

Burn the fancy candle.
Wear the special-occasion dress.
Pop the good bottle.
Scribble *Hurry slowly* on the first page
of your leather-bound notebook.
Gorge on your pearls,
your cashmere, your silks.
Use the high-end eyeshadow
until the silver pan winks back.
Baptize your wrists in Baccarat Rouge,
a little extra for the collar.
Devour your nice things—
don't let the best go cold on your plate.
The anticipation of living
is empty calories,
and you were meant to be full.

MY GRANDMOTHER SAYS WINE IS BASICALLY A WHOLE FOOD

After Joy Sullivan

Which is another way to say: Don't take life too seriously.
Get your antioxidants from a glass of red.
Cut curtain bangs with sewing scissors
and grow them out in time for spring.
Don't stress about what you look like in photos—
ten years from now you'll think you were beautiful.
Learn to knit scarves for loved ones, not as a side hustle.
Pepper wildflower seeds on the front lawn.
Spread your toes in the sand on a weekday.
Put down the self-improvement book
and read a sunscreen paperback.
Wear your brightest colors in a room of beige,
a cardinal in a winter field.
Bake a chocolate cake because you want to.
Fill your life with stories you'll want to remember
when you're long in the tooth.
Laugh about how absurd
and astonishing it all is.
Rub it between your palms like sage.
Swirl it, thick as honey, in your glass.
Let it stain your lips,
your tongue.

FIREFLIES

Three decades on this borrowed blue jewel,
in this woman-shaped skin,
and I have yet to see a firefly.
I've spent years scanning
summer's freckled shoulders,
and I'm realizing now
that if my existence were a single day,
I'd only now be getting dressed—
my first cup of coffee still hot
on the bathroom counter
while I wipe wandering dots
of mascara from my upper eyelid.
The sky of my life hasn't even begun
to violet yet—so many evenings
stretch out before me like open arms,
sun climbing slow as a hymn.
When my honeyed dusk
drags its belly across the backyard,
maybe I will have seen them
with my own eyes,
or maybe the sun will leave me
barefoot in the grass.
But what a miracle it would be,
to leave this body and still believe
in a light I've never seen,
to trust that it's always flickering
just beyond.

HERE'S WHAT I'VE LEARNED AFTER THIRTY-ONE YEARS

That to watch the yielding plum of my body
ripen is the privilege of my life / that forgiveness
isn't a single act but a muscle you learn
to stretch / to salt the pasta water until it tastes
like the ocean / to stoke the loves in your life
like small, steady flames / to tend to grief
like an overgrown garden / that it matters to learn
the names of the trees and flowers / that you do not
need to earn rest / to butter the bread all the way
to the edges / that joy pools in the bends carved
by sorrow / that silence can be both weapon
and balm / that the smallest rituals—the salt,
the flame, the bread—are the point of it all /
that the world, despite everything,
is still a soft place to land.

THE LILACS ARE IN BLOOM

and once again I am reminded
how every perfect thing—
the tiny, four-petaled florets,
watercolored together in dribbling
lavender plumes; the sweet, milky
scent of my daughter's newborn
breath, the robin's-egg weight
of her so impossibly light on my chest;
the flutter of inspiration, breathtaking
as a butterfly migration, passing
through only when you're lucky
enough to find yourself in its path—
is perfect not in spite of its brevity
but because of it,
because it urges us to pay attention,
to hold it with two trembling hands,
to feel the beauty and the loss
all at once.

FINAL ACT

My grandmother once told me
the reason she got thyroid cancer
was because she never spoke up for herself,
as if each withheld word lodged itself
in her throat, splintered like chicken bones.
But it wasn't the cancer that took her,
or even the starvation and dehydration.
In the end, she took the low candle with its
dying flame between her potter's hands
and pinched it out with two firm fingers,
which is to say, after a lifetime of swallowing
her own desire, in her final act,
she struck a bell and sang.

ON LEAVING THE FLOWERS TOO LONG IN THE VASE

I can't decide which part of me
lets the flowers rot—
the one that can't bear endings
or the one that can't be bothered
with them. I tell myself
I'll throw them out tomorrow,
and instead I watch each petal
darken by degrees,
water gone cloudy and rank
as time itself. Maybe I like
the idea of letting things end
without forcing grace upon them,
to let the flower be the full thing—
beautiful and withered, fragrant
and fetid. Maybe I like
the idea of being alive
enough to ruin.

DID YOU KNOW WE LITERALLY GET ONE WILD AND PRECIOUS LIFE?

After Chloe Laws

And you expect me to care about spreadsheets,
emails, and whether or not to eat dairy?
To spend my days obsessed with how small
I can make my body instead of how fully
I can live inside it? When did it become normal
to worry more about what others think of me
than what *I* think of me? To grind until my bones
scatter like dust in the wind? You can keep
the *busybossbitchsupermom* posed perfectly
on her shelf. I want a life of stupid ease.
Give me slow. Unhurried. Unbothered.
Give me warm sourdough with an extra pat of butter
and the well-fed body of an ancient Greek goddess.
I want to float through my one precious life.
To kiss it soft and slow on the lips—
trace its laugh lines with my thumbs
and tell it: *I love you. I love you.*

I AM A LITTLE BIT IN LOVE

with the woman at the grocery store,
her wide brim cinching sun hat
and phone folio case; with the man
at gymnastics pulling his son's hair
into a ponytail; with the waitress who keeps
calling me babe; with the repairman
who took his shoes off without asking;
with the catcalling guy on the bicycle
who nicknamed me summer; with the older
lady in the airport who asked if I was off
to college; with the girl at the market
who kissed her baby doll's fingers.
And I wonder how many times I've been
the stranger someone loved like a blink,
like a glint, like the zap of a current
that runs everywhere all at once.

ANNIE DILLARD SAYS "HOW WE SPEND OUR DAYS IS, OF COURSE, HOW WE SPEND OUR LIVES"

and I want to spend my life
like I spend Sunday mornings—
barefoot in a kitchen lit up like an apricot,
my baby sticky with strawberry jam,
the sky forgetting how to be gray.
I want to write something beautiful
or furious,
to touch the tops of my daughter's ears,
to scrub the counters,
to kiss my love at the stove.
I want an hour to read a book,
and another to stare out the window—
at the birds, at nothing, at everything.
I want to bake a loaf of bread
and forget the laundry in the machine,
to raise my voice,
to say sorry,
to be forgiven.
I want to open the windows
when it rains,
to let the day undo me a little,
a tired trace of mascara beneath my eyes.
I want to notice the light
slanting across the floor,
the way my daughter's hair curls
at the nape after a bath,
the quiet click of the oven cooling—
all the small, invisible ways
the ordinary becomes holy.

ACKNOWLEDGMENTS

Thank you to the editors of the following journals where these poems first appeared:

Only Poems: "Bad Luck," "Sky Rats," "First Impressions," "Might Should," "Wild Indulgence," "Let Me Tell You How a Stitch Only Snaps When It's Worn Too Thin," "Final Act"

Central Avenue Poetry Prize 2025: "Tender Flesh"

Ninth Heaven: "I Am Eating a Handful of Figs," "The Dogwood," "Humans Are the Only Species Known to Blush," "A Broken Rule," "Even Here," "Stones Beneath the Sand," "Orogenesis," "The Lilacs Are in Bloom"

Gather: "My Daughter"

"To the Woman at the Patisserie Who Turned Down Cake Because She Was 'Trying to Be Good'" was written for, and anthologized in, *If You Ever: Poems Inspired by Kim Addonizio.*

"My Grandmother Is Dead and I'm Standing in Line to Buy Chicken" was awarded second place in *The Black Horse Review* poetry contest.

Thank you to the editors at *Only Poems* for nominating "Might Should" for Best of the Net and for consistently championing my work; to The Substack Post for featuring "I Didn't Know My Grandmother Was a Poet"; and to Hannah Monsour and Zoe Branch at Poking Around Podcast for featuring "The Things We Leave Behind."

Special thanks to Megan Johansen, quoted in "We Grieve in Accordance with How Much We Love"; to my beta readers, whose feedback and encouragement were invaluable; to all the friends, mentors, teachers, and readers who remind me constantly that art is never made alone; and to my sister, Willow, who provided childcare (and emotional support) throughout the making of this book.

I'm especially grateful to Michelle, publisher at Central Avenue, for her incredible generosity and belief in my work, and to editors Beau, Jessica, and Molly for their insight, patience, and attention to detail that helped shape this book.

Finally, thank you to my husband, Joe, who reads every single one of my poems and believes in me more than anyone ever has (often including myself); and to my daughter, Lily, whose joy and curiosity remind me daily what all of this is about. I love you both all the world.

Elise Powers received a BA in English literature from Western Washington University. Her poems reflect on identity, womanhood, and the ordinary moments that make up a life. Her work has appeared in literary magazines and anthologies including *Gather* and *Only Poems*, and has been shortlisted for the *Central Avenue Poetry Prize*, awarded second place in the *Black Horse Review Poetry Contest*, and nominated for the *Best of the Net Anthology*. She lives in Seattle with her husband and daughter, where she writes, collects sea glass, and savors life's tender joys. Find more of her work on Instagram @elisepowerspoet and on Substack at Two Raw Sugars.